VERA
The Alien Hunter

2

Story by   Jason Wilburn & Casey Kim

Illustrations by   Seungjun Park & Bioh Kang

e **future**

Characters

Bad alien

Bigfoot

Vera's mom

Vera's dad

Zarbo

Rameonie

Luca

Vera

Coming Up!

From Luca's Mission

STORY 1

Luca's Mission

PASTONIA

MOON-MEAT

YETINON

-272°C

MULA²

People GRAPH

e·future

looking for

people

police officer

train

air

gold

water

Go to page 19 for Activity 1.

believe   keep   police   president

big

small

travel

Go to page 20 for Activity 2.

ropes

size

strong

weak

crashed

hair

tall

Go to page 21
for Activity 3.

different first many work

Go to page 22
for Activity 4.

Activity 1

For page 4 ~ page 7

1 Find and circle the words.

1

g	e	l	a	t	v
w	a	t	e	r	b
d	e	h	e	a	i
l	e	a	a	i	r
g	o	l	d	n	s

2

3

4

2 Circle T (True) or F (False).

1 Luca is from outer space. T / F

2 Luca is a space teacher. T / F

3 Most people know that Luca is an alien. T / F

4 All aliens are bad. T / F

5 Some bad aliens want to eat people. T / F

19

① Match.

| keep | travel | president | believe |

② Circle the correct words.

1 Vera wants to tell (the police / her dad) about the aliens.

2 The (president / police officer) knows about the aliens.

3 Vera must keep (Earth / space) safe.

4 Luca travels all over the (Earth / galaxy).

5 Aliens from Mula 2 are very (big / small).

Activity 3

① Write the words.

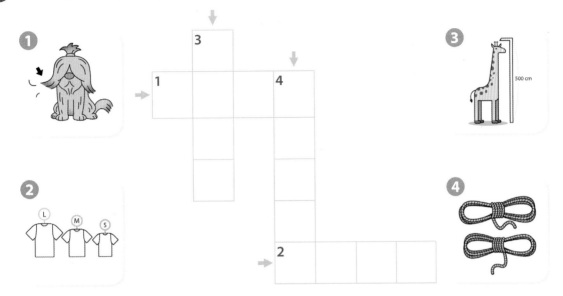

② Choose and write.

alien hunter	believe	strong	weak

1 I'm not _____, Luca.

2 Some aliens are very _____.
Rameonie can't hold her space blaster.

3 Really? Maybe I can be an _____.

4 You need to _____ in yourself.

① Choose and write.

| different | many | first | work |

1   2   3   4

_____ _____ _____ _____

② Write the sentences in the correct order.

1   (my alien/ Look / at / hunting gear / .)

_____

2   (can't / You / that / fight / with / .)

_____

3   (we / What / do / should / ?)

_____

4   (real alien / We'll / hunting gear / you / get / .)

_____

Key Words

Check the words you learned.

p. 7	☐ air	p. 5	☐ looking for	p. 13	☐ strong
p. 9	☐ believe	p. 17	☐ many	p. 15	☐ tall
p. 11	☐ big	p. 5	☐ people	p. 5	☐ train
p. 15	☐ crashed	p. 9	☐ police	p. 11	☐ travel
p. 17	☐ different	p. 5	☐ police officer	p. 7	☐ water
p. 17	☐ first	p. 9	☐ president	p. 13	☐ weak
p. 7	☐ gold	p. 13	☐ rope	p. 17	☐ work
p. 15	☐ hair	p. 13	☐ size		
p. 9	☐ keep	p. 11	☐ small		

Useful Expressions

Check the expressions you learned.

p. 16	☐ I trust you, Luca.	p. 9	☐ It's up to you, Vera.
p. 15	☐ I think so.	p. 14	☐ Tell me about strong aliens.
p. 10	☐ I don't think so, Luca.	p. 16	☐ Believe in yourself, Vera.
p. 6	☐ I can't believe it!	p. 16	☐ Trust me.
p. 16	☐ I'll work hard.	p. 5	☐ Are you ready?
p. 18	☐ It's all junk.	p. 5	☐ Why me?
p. 4	☐ My name's Luca.	p. 17	☐ What's wrong?
p. 7	☐ Luca, that sounds scary.	p. 17	☐ What do we do first?
p. 14	☐ That looks like Bigfoot!	p. 18	☐ What should we do?

Coming Up! From Getting Ready for the Worst

Vera can't stop the evil aliens.
She needs new alien hunting gear.
Luca isn't worried. He has a plan.
Where will Vera find new alien hunting gear?

Getting Ready for the Worst

far away   gear   nearby   signal

leads

pointing

woods

Go to page 41 for Activity 5.

empty

hand

touch

wall

lights

mountain

spaceship

Go to page 42 for Activity 6.

perfect

put … on

room

start

button   rest   suit

Go to page 43 for Activity 7.

glad   lots of   old   secret

Go to page 44
for Activity 8.

① Choose and write.

lead	woods	far away	nearby

1 _____

2 _____

3 _____

4 _____

② Circle the correct words.

1 Vera's gear is (bad / good).

2 Luca's UFO is (far away / nearby).

3 Luca wants to find some gear (far away / nearby).

4 The signal leads Luca and Vera to the (woods / park).

5 Bigfoot (doesn't live / lives) in the cave.

Activity 6

1 Find and circle the words.

z	e	m	p	t	y
y	w	r	q	o	l
h	a	n	d	u	t
r	l	a	l	c	e
k	l	t	p	h	n

2 Circle T (True) or F (False).

1 Vera likes to play in the big cave.   T / F

2 There is a spaceship under the mountain.   T / F

3 The spaceship is new and clean.   T / F

4 The lights work on the spaceship.   T / F

5 Luca thinks the spaceship is dangerous.   T / F

Activity 7

1 Write the words.

2 Choose and write.

practice	button	suit	rest

What's this _____ for?
1

Look! I'm in the air!

Oh no! I can't control this _____.
2

You need more _____.
3

But, not today. Let's go home and _____.
4

Activity 8

① Match.

| lots of | glad | secret | old |

② Write the sentences in the correct order.

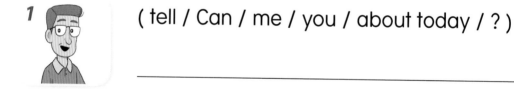

1 (tell / Can / me / you / about today / ?)

_____

2 (the cave / a spaceship / in / There's / .)

_____

3 (a / What / story / silly / .)

_____

Key Words

Check the words you learned.

p. 37 ☐ button	p. 33 ☐ mountain	p. 27 ☐ signal
p. 31 ☐ empty	p. 27 ☐ nearby	p. 33 ☐ spaceship
p. 27 ☐ far away	p. 39 ☐ old	p. 35 ☐ start
p. 27 ☐ gear	p. 35 ☐ perfect	p. 37 ☐ suit
p. 39 ☐ glad	p. 29 ☐ pointing	p. 31 ☐ touch
p. 31 ☐ hand	p. 35 ☐ put … on	p. 31 ☐ wall
p. 29 ☐ lead	p. 37 ☐ rest	p. 29 ☐ woods
p. 33 ☐ light	p. 35 ☐ room	
p. 39 ☐ lots of	p. 39 ☐ secret	

Useful Expressions

Check the expressions you learned.

p. 26 ☐ I'm sure of it.	p. 28 ☐ Let's follow the signal.
p. 31 ☐ It looks like a hand.	p. 33 ☐ Let's check it out.
p. 30 ☐ It doesn't look scary.	p. 34 ☐ Well, let's see.
p. 33 ☐ Of course. Come on!	p. 35 ☐ Let's start with this.
p. 38 ☐ I can't tell you, Dad.	p. 36 ☐ Let's go home and rest.
p. 39 ☐ I'm glad to hear that.	p. 33 ☐ Are you sure?
p. 32 ☐ Look at that!	p. 38 ☐ Vera, can you tell me about today?
p. 35 ☐ Put this on.	p. 31 ☐ Why don't you touch it?
p. 29 ☐ Let's go in there.	p. 36 ☐ What's this button for?

Coming Up! From All Is Safe

The old spaceship is full of great gear.
That will help Vera.
But, Vera isn't ready yet.
She has a lot to learn.
Can Luca teach her?

STORY 3

All Is Safe

busy

give

planet

protect

last

live

vacation

Go to page 63
for Activity 9.

batteries broken fly home

danger

flashing

sky

Go to page 64
for Activity 10.

Imagine a shell around you.

Your suit will block the balls.

TATATATA

Your mind controls it. Believe in yourself.

POW! POW!

BZZZZ...

WHAM!

Wow! I did it! I have a shell around me!

armor

around

block

shell

aim

push

shoot

Go to page 65
for Activity 11.

bring

forget

necklace

pretty

Go to page 66
for Activity 12.

① Choose and write.

| vacation | last | give | busy |

1  2 3 4

_____ _____ _____ _____

② Who says this? Read and match.

1

Wake up!
It's time for breakfast.

2

I may be small.
I may be weak.
But, I will fight and protect
this planet!

3

So, you are the alien hunter.
You are small and weak.
Just give me the Earth.

❶ Find and circle the words.

z	e	h	s	h	y
b	r	o	k	e	n
c	f	m	y	m	g
v	l	e	b	a	r
d	a	n	g	e	r

❷ Circle **T** (True) or **F** (False).

1 The lights still work on the old spaceship.　　T / F

2 The spaceship has special batteries.　　T / F

3 The spaceship can fly.　　T / F

4 Vera and Luca can scan the cave

in the control room.　　T / F

5 A flashing red light on the spaceship is good.　T / F

Activity 11

1 Choose and write.

| armor | shoot | aim | push |

1 _____

2 _____

3 _____

4 _____

2 Choose and write.

| block | mind | shell | yourself |

Your suit will _____ the balls. Imagine
                        1
a _____ around you. Your _____
      2   3
controls it. Believe in _____.
                             4

Wow! I did it.

① Match.

| necklace | forget | bring | pretty |

② Circle the correct words.

1 Vera's (hands / mind) can control the gear.

2 Vera is (excited / scared) to be an alien hunter.

3 Luca gives Vera a pretty (necklace / ring).

4 Luca and Vera are going (home / to school) to rest.

5 Luca and Vera will come to the spaceship again

(after / before) school tomorrow.

Key Words

Check the words you learned.

p. 59 ☐ aim	p. 55 ☐ flashing	p. 61 ☐ pretty
p. 57 ☐ armor	p. 53 ☐ fly	p. 49 ☐ protect
p. 57 ☐ around	p. 61 ☐ forget	p. 59 ☐ push
p. 53 ☐ battery	p. 49 ☐ give	p. 57 ☐ shell
p. 57 ☐ block	p. 53 ☐ home	p. 59 ☐ shoot
p. 61 ☐ bring	p. 51 ☐ last	p. 55 ☐ sky
p. 53 ☐ broken	p. 51 ☐ live	p. 51 ☐ vacation
p. 49 ☐ busy	p. 61 ☐ necklace	
p. 55 ☐ danger	p. 49 ☐ planet	

Useful Expressions

Check the expressions you learned.

p. 49 ☐ It's time for breakfast.	p. 55 ☐ We need to practice.
p. 59 ☐ That's right.	p. 62 ☐ We should go home.
p. 60 ☐ This is so cool!	p. 59 ☐ You can do it.
p. 55 ☐ I'm ready to learn.	p. 56 ☐ Get ready!
p. 58 ☐ I don't understand.	p. 58 ☐ Be careful with it.
p. 62 ☐ I should get some rest.	p. 51 ☐ Say "hello" to Bigfoot for me.
p. 60 ☐ I won't forget, Luca.	p. 60 ☐ Don't forget.
p. 57 ☐ Wow! I did it!	p. 50 ☐ What will you do today?
p. 49 ☐ We have a busy day.	p. 61 ☐ What a pretty necklace!

Next Book

Next Time — From Back to School

Vera's summer vacation is over.
She needs to go back to school.
But danger is coming!
Is Vera ready?
Can she save the Earth?

Theme Song

Theme Song

Vera!
Earth is depending on you, Vera.
The alien hunter.
You will be there, and you'll save the day.

It's like a story.
One made up in my head.
How do I know that all of this is real?

You have to trust me.
You have to do your best.
I'll help you learn the things you need to know.

But what if I'm not strong enough?
But what if I'm too small?
I don't know what I can do, but I'll try!
And you will succeed!

Vera!
Earth is depending on you, Vera.
The alien hunter.
You will be there, and you'll save the day.

It's not a story.
It's not just in my head.
I will do great if I can just believe.

Yes, I will trust you.
I'll learn all I can learn.
I will succeed if I believe in me.

So what if I'm not strong enough?
So what if I'm too small?
I will do the best I can, and I know that I will
succeed!

Vera!
Earth is depending on you, Vera.
The alien hunter.
You will be there, and you'll save the day.

Vera!
Earth is depending on you, Vera.
The alien hunter.
You will be there!
Now you'll save the day.

Grammar in Book 2

Verb Tenses	· Present simple · Present continuous · Future: will
Verb Forms and Sentence Patterns	· Affirmatives, negatives · Interrogatives: wh-questions, yes/no questions · Imperatives
Modal Verbs	· Can: ability, request · Must, have to: personal obligation · Will: future
Others	· Articles: a/an, the · Possessive adjectives · Let's ~